the magnificent scenery, outdoor lifestyle, and unique homes of an American treasure

Idaho
a great place to live

PUBLISHED BY RHINO BOOKS • BOISE, IDAHO
ART DIRECTION AND DESIGN BY ED GUTHERO

principal photography by Steve Bly, Mark Lisk, David Stoecklein, and Tim Brown

additional photography by Phil McClain, Quicksilver Studios, Lisa Brown, John Baker, Kirk Keough, Stan Sinclair, Glenn Oakley, Ed Guthero, Fred Lindholm, Joseph Henry Wythe, Roger Wade, Alan Weintraub, Alan Bisson, Tom Stewart, Kevin Syms, and by the courtesy of the owners of the unique homes, resorts, golf courses, and institutions featured in this book.

Editorial Assistance: Jackson Quast, Maureen Halloran/Calliope Communications, Ed Guthero; Design Assistance: Michelle C. Petz

IDAHO LIFESTYLE SECTION BEGINS ON PAGE 3
(UNIQUE IDAHO RESORTS AND GOLF COURSES SECTION BEGINS ON PAGE 73)

IDAHO UNIQUE HOMES BEGIN ON PAGE 84

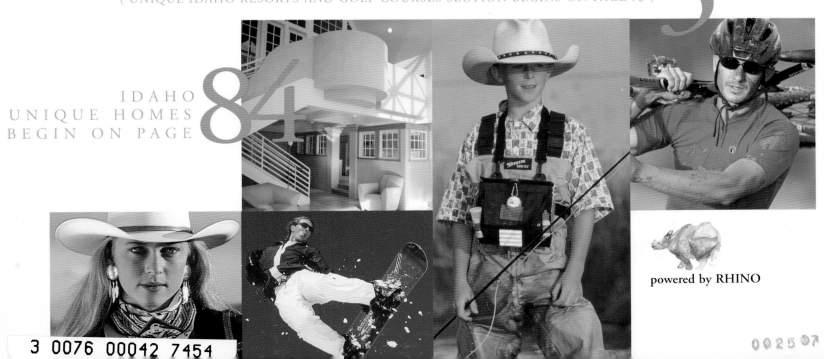

powered by RHINO

002507

1

Uniques Homes of Idaho
The magnificent scenery, unique homes, and outdoor
lifestyle of an American treasure

Copyright © 2002 by Rhino Books and Ron Wilks

All Rights Reserved

ISBN 0-615-11967-0

Photos: David Stoecklein

UNIQUE HOMES OF
Idaho

Published by Rhino Books and Ron Wilks
P.O. Box 16348, Boise, ID 83715
www.RhinoBooks.net

Printed by Sung In Printing America, Inc. / Korea
Color separations by Graphics Avenue, Boise, ID

Cover and book jacket design: Ed Guthero
Cover and book jacket photos: Quicksilver Studios, Phil McClain, Steve
Bly, David Stoecklein, Ed Guthero, Mark Lisk, Kirk Keough

To obtain limited edition fine art prints or use of many of the images in
this book go to www. bigtreeseditions.com

The publisher would like to thank the various photographers, architects,
builders, home owners, realtors, resort and lodge personnel, and others
whose information and images appear in this publication.

"I never knew a man who felt self-important in the morning after spending the night in the open on an Idaho mountainside under a starstudded summer sky. Save some time in your lives for the outdoors, where you can be witness to the wonders of God."

Frank Church, former U. S. Senator from Idaho

Message from
The Governor

Whether you live in Idaho or are just visiting, you already know about Idaho's spectacular natural beauty and outstanding quality of life. Towering peaks, thundering rivers, pristine lakes, lush forests, incredible fishing and endless trails are just the beginning.

But you might not know that Idaho is also one of the best places in the country to locate your company. With our low business costs, highly-educated and motivated work-force and business-friendly government, expanding or relocating your business in Idaho can help make your company more profitable.

No matter what route your travels take you, Idaho's friendly people, unspoiled scenery, a well-preserved past, and varied recreational activities and cultural events await you and your family.

Governor Dirk Kempthorne

"Rhino Books is proud to present the state of Idaho through the visual presentation of some of the most beautiful landscapes, recreation scenes, and unique homes found throughout the state. This book is divided into two sections:

The first features Idaho's magnificent natural beauty, varied lifestyles, and a contemporary overview of this mountain west jewel; the second section takes you on a guided tour of some of Idaho's most distinctive and original homes.

We wish to thank the Idaho Department of Commerce / Idaho Division of Tourism Development, the homeowners who graciously opened their doors to make this special publication possible, and all the Idaho photographers who wake each morning knowing they will be blessed with yet another Idaho vista.

The lengendary writer and former Idaho resident Ernest Hemingway said it best: "A great place to live, Idaho."

— *Ron Wilks, Publisher*
RHINO BOOKS

Idaho is known worldwide for it's spectacular whitewater rapids.

Idaho

Area: 83,557 square miles
Population (2000): 1,293,953
Capitol and largest city: Boise
Statehood: July 3, 1890
Highest point: Borah Peak—12,662 ft
Lowest point: Snake River—710 ft
Nickname: Gem State
Motto: Esto Perpetua—It Is Perpetual
State bird: Mountain Bluebird
State flower: Syringa
State tree: White Pine

- Sixty-three percent of Idaho is public land, and at 2.3 million acres, the Frank Church River of No Return Wilderness is the largest wilderness area in the 48 contiguous states.

- The Salmon River is the nation's longest free-flowing river that heads and flows within a single state. Because of its difficult passage, it's also known as the "River of No Return."

- Sacajawea, a Lemhi Shoshone from what is now the Montana/Idaho border, guided Merriwether Lewis and William Clark through Northern Idaho to the mouth of the Columbia River drainage. Today, Highway 12 follows the Lewis and Clark trail along the Lochsa (pronounced "lock-saw"), Clearwater and Snake Rivers.

- Five pioneer trails, including the Oregon Trail and the California Trail cross Southern Idaho. Wagon ruts are still visible in the rugged terrain.

- The Nautilus, the first engineering prototype of a nuclear submarine, was built and tested in 1953 in the arid Snake River Plain near Arco.

- Almost 85% of all commercial trout sold in the U.S. comes from the Hagerman Valley, near Twin Falls.

- On August 13, 1896, Butch Cassidy—a.k.a George Leroy Parker—stole $7,165 from the bank in Montpelier, Idaho. Allegedly, the money was to hire a lawyer for his partner Matt Warner, who was awaiting trial for murder in Utah.

- The Snake River Birds of Prey Natural Area is home to the largest concentration of nesting raptors in Northern America.

Thousands of visitors visit this site near Kuna every spring and summer.

- Wilson Butte Cave near Twin Falls was excavated in 1959 and found to contain bison and antelope bones, arrowheads and other artifacts that were carbon-dated to be 14,500 years old. This makes them "among the oldest definitely dated artifacts in the New World."

- Craters of the Moon National Monument in Southeast Idaho contains nearly 40 separate lava flows, some formed as recently as 250 years ago. The otherworldly area was used as a training ground for early astronauts. June's lavish display of wildflowers adds to the surreal landscape.

- The Silver Valley in Northern Idaho is one of the top 10 mining districts in the world. It has produced more than $4 billion in precious metals since 1884.

- Appropriately named The Gem State, Idaho produces 72 types of precious and semi-precious stones, some of which can be found nowhere else in the world. One of the largest diamonds ever found in the U.S., nearly 20 carats, was discovered near McCall.

- The Port of Lewiston exports millions of bushels of grain down the Snake and Columbia Rivers for overseas shipment, classifying it as a non-coastal city with a seaport.

- The Statehouse in Boise and dozens of other buildings in the city are geothermally heated with underground hot springs. In fact, Idaho is well-plumbed with hot springs, both public and private.

Come Find Idaho

Come find waterfalls that reach to the sky
And flirt with trout in a clear blue stream
Discover legendary resorts or rustic guest ranches
Hidden in pristine secluded forests of pine
Glide down mountains blanketed in powder
Tell ghost stories under a starry sky
Where the only rush hours are on rivers
Come find Idaho.

– Idaho Department of Commerce

Idaho is a land of stately mountain ranges. At left: Snow-capped Borah and Leatherman peaks in the Lost River Range.

Photos: Mark Lisk

Idaho and the outdoors are synonymous.
Photographer David Stoecklein captures a panorama
of outdoor adventure in the recreational paradise of
Sun Valley.

freedom, challenge, renewal . . . the land lights a fire within us

11

IDAHO Geography

*I*daho is a state rich in geographical extremes from high desert to towering peaks, an expanse of timberlands, scenic lakes, roaring rivers, and breathtaking gorges. It is a land that is largely unspoiled with the largest wilderness area in the contiguous United States. Idaho is about 45 miles wide in the northern Panhandle and then broadens to about 310 miles south of the Bitterroot Range. The Snake River, which boasts the deepest river gorge in the North American Continent with Hells Canyon at 7,900 feet deep, flows in a great arc across southern Idaho. The river has been harnessed to produce hydroelectric power and to reclaim vast areas of dry but fertile land. To the north of the Snake River Valley, in central and north central Idaho, are the massive Sawtooth Mountains and the Salmon River Mountains, which shelter magnificent wilderness areas, including the Frank Church River of No Return Wilderness, the Selway Bitterroot Wilderness Area and the Idaho Primitive Area.

Tremendous expanses of national forests cover approximately two fifths of the state in the central and north central regions. Idaho's jagged peaks include Mount Borah, which is 12,662 feet high, and the magnificent Sawtooth Mountains where the headwaters of the Salmon River and over 300 alpine lakes lie in pristine beauty. The state also contains Craters of the Moon National Monument that contains nearly 40 separate lava flows, and which was used as a training ground for early astronauts. There's even a protected grove of ancient cedars at Upper Priest Lake.

Idaho is considered a superb fish and game preserve with its many lakes such as Lake Pend Oreille, Lake Coeur d'Alene, and Priest Lake, and its untainted rivers like the Salmon and the Clearwater, as well as the state's mountain areas. It offers rich experiences to those who enjoy camping, hiking, hunting, fishing and other outdoor activities. The state's climate ranges from hot summers in the arid southern basins to cold, snowy winters in the high wilderness areas of central and northern Idaho.

"A great place to live, Idaho" *–Ernest Hemingway*

At left: White pines decorate the rocky shoreline of Goat Lake in the Sawtooth Wilderness.

Regions
Northern
North Central
Southwestern
South Central
Central
Eastern

NORTHERN
Idaho

Northern

The "Panhandle" region of North Idaho has 2,000 miles of rivers and 140 lakes, giving this area the greatest concentration of lakes of any western state. Densely forested mountains and lush green valleys frame the pristine lakes that teem with wild fish.

"...If you push me up against a wall as to my favorite spot, I would probably answer the Rocky Mountains of the West, around Idaho. There's something about coming around a corner and seeing a meadow full of wildflowers." –Charles Kurault, CBS journalist

Lake Coeur d'Alene

Pristine Lake Coeur d'Alene was formed by glaciers during the Ice Age. This international resort destination is a spectacular place for all ages to enjoy sailing, water-skiing and fishing while enjoying nature's backdrop. Resorts and modern amenities are on the north shore in the city of Coeur d'Alene, a recent recipient of an "All America City" award.

Priest Lake

Priest Lake offers plenty for the camper and fisherman. World-class Mackinaw trout and kokanee salmon have been pulled from its waters. The remote beauty of the lake rivals the more developed Lake Tahoe, and the nearby Roosevelt Grove of Ancient Cedars contains trees over 200 years old.

Lake Pend Oreille

The largest of Idaho's lakes, Lake Pend Oreille near Sandpoint has a well-deserved reputation as a fisherman's paradise. Fourteen species of game fish inhabit its waters, including kokanee, largemouth bass and bluegill. The largest Kamloops trout in the world and a 32-pound Dolly Varden came from this lake.

Spirit Lake

Spirit Lake is North Idaho's highest small lake and one of only two lakes in the world that has a sealed bottom. Four and a half miles long, the lake is over 100 feet deep and boasts twelve miles of beautiful shoreline. The skyline is dominated by the majestic Selkirk Mountains to the north and west.

At left: Northern Idaho's majestic beauty ranges from stately mountains to the subtle pleasures of flowers in a dense woodland.

Sandpoint

The town of Sandpoint is located on spectacular Lake Pend Oreille. Settled in the 1880s, it became an important logging, milling and rail center. Today, it is a thriving resort community with lively visual and performing arts, shopping and nightlife.

Wallace

Wallace is one of the few places where the entire town is listed on the National Register of Historic Places. It has one of the best collections of turn-of-the-century architecture in the Pacific Northwest. Several buildings date back to 1890, when a fire destroyed most of the mining town.

Below: (top) Trout are abundant in Idaho's rivers and streams. (bottom) English setter hunting dog retrieving chuckers.

Photos: Mark Lisk, Kirk Keough (fish)

At left : Copper Falls in the Purcell Mountains of North Idaho.
Below: Coeur d'Alene's waterfront resort hotel and five star golf course, featuring a floating hole, is an outstanding vacation spot in North Idaho.

NORTH CENTRAL
Idaho

North Central Idaho invokes peace with its verdant vistas and inspires reveries on nature's wonders with its geographical extremes.

Nez Perce

The Nez Perce tribe of Native Americans has a legend that the earth was created in Northern Idaho—at a place near Kamiah. The animals, the spirits and mankind all lived in harmonious simplicity. Today, Kamiah is still part of the Nez Perce reservation.

Hell's Canyon

At 7,900 feet Hell's Canyon is the deepest river gorge in North America. In some places, the canyon walls plunge more than a mile to sandy riverbanks below. The mighty Seven Devils Mountains crest over the gorge for an awe-inspiring sight.

Whitewater Rafting

Whitewater rafting is a fine art in North Central Idaho. From Riggins, you can float the Main Salmon or the Lower Salmon Rivers. The particularly intrepid enjoy kayaking.

Moscow

Moscow (pronounced "moss-coh") is the seat of Latah County—the only county in Idaho established by an Act of Congress. Founded in 1888, the town boasts the University of Idaho and incredible architecture that chronicles its long and varied history.

Lewiston

At 739 feet, it boasts the lowest elevation in the state—meaning that its climate is especially mild, even in the middle of winter. Conveniently located between the Snake and Clearwater Rivers, it has long been a natural center of commerce. Lewiston was also the state's first town to be incorporated.

Orofino

Due to the inflow of settlers and the construction of the railroad up river, Orofino's town site got its start in 1898. The name was taken from a gold rush town called "Oro Fino" (meaning fine gold) that was located near Pierce and later burned down. Just outside Orofino is Dworshak Reservoir, a 53-mile-long lake created by Dworshak Dam, which is the largest straight axis dam in North America.

At left: Lupine blooms on the White Bird battlefield of the Nez Perce war.

Below: Farm land in the rolling hills of Idaho's Palouse Country. Top right: Wild Sheep Rapid, Hell's Canyon on the Snake River. Idaho's famed Hell's Canyon is North America's deepest river gorge. Bottom right: Portion of the Snake River near Hell's Canyon.

SOUTHWESTERN
Idaho

*A*lpine lakes, velvety green mountains and the tallest desert sand dunes in North America offer splendid geographical diversity while the Snake River arcs across the southern regions of the state. Southwestern Idaho is home to the capitol city of Boise, which Outside Magazine named one of American's ten best cities in which to live.

Boise—Idaho's Capitol

One of the Pacific Northwest's fastest growing high-tech cities, Boise is a vibrant community where you can ski in the morning, play golf in the afternoon, and attend live theater at night.

Photos: Steve Bensten, c/o World Center for Birds of Prey. Opposite: Mark Lisk

Boise is also home to Boise State University and the city's centerpiece is a 25-mile greenbelt along the Boise River.

Nampa/Caldwell

A scant fifteen miles from Boise, the Nampa/Caldwell area is one of the most agriculturally productive in the United States. In fact, many of Idaho's famous potatoes are grown here.

Nampa hosts the annual Snake River Stampede, while Caldwell hosts the Caldwell Night Rodeo—two of America's most respected rodeos.

Bruneau Sand Dunes

The tallest sand dunes in North America rise to 470 feet high above small lakes near Mountain Home. This state park features fishing, camping, bird watching and Idaho's only public observatory.

Snake River Birds of Prey

Established in 1971, this area is home to North America's densest population of nesting raptors, and covers 483,000 acres along 80 miles of the Snake River. Eagles, hawks, falcons, owls and vultures sail on the unique updrafts and wind currents of the area, and raise their young in the canyon.

McCall

McCall is built on the shores of the beautiful Payette Lake, and the forestlands surrounding the town provide excellent fishing in over 30 lakes and 1,400 miles of streams. Brundage Mountain Ski Resort is noted for its abundant snow. The McCall February Winter Carnival features ice sculptures, parades, and festivities. Surprisingly, McCall remains one of Idaho's best-kept secrets.

At left: Aplomado falcon, one of the residents of Idaho's famed Snake River Birds of Prey Center. At right: A captivating scene of splendid color and light at the Bruneau River Canyon, situated in the Owyhee Desert of Southwest Idaho.

Above: Inflatable kayaking on Idaho's wild and scenic rivers. At right: Whitewater rafting on the Payette River system near Boise.

Challenge the spirit of adventure within.

Photos: Mark Lisk. Top: c/o Idaho Birds of Prey, Art Wolfe

Above (main): Rock climbing is another of Idaho's many exciting outdoor adventures. Top right: The Birds of Prey Raptor Sanctuary is not only home to birds native to the region, but also raptors foreign to the area, such as the rare California Condor and Harpy Eagle pictured above.

Below: Elephant shaped rock in the Owyhee Desert.
Opposite right: Windblown patterns at Bruneau Dunes State Park.

Photos: Mark Lisk

Above: Wild horses roam the deserts of Owyhee county.
At right: A hard-working Idaho cowboy.

26

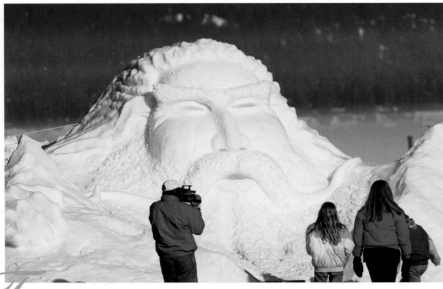

*T*he annual McCall Winter Carnival features impressive ice sculptures as a major part of the festivities. At right: A field of shooting stars splash a wave of color across a field near McCall. Below: A harbour view of Payette Lake, McCall.

Photos: Steve Bly, Opposite: Mark Lisk

Boise offers an abundant lifestyle. Below: Teens cycle in the foothills overlooking the city. At right: A closeup of exuberant runners from the annual Women's Fitness Celebration run. Opposite page, top left: Thousands of Women's Fitness Celebration participants stream down Capitol Boulevard.

Biking Photo: Mark Lisk, Bogus Basin: Steve Bly, others: c/o Women's Fitness Celebration, Boise River Festival, Kirk Keogh

The annual Boise River Festival draws tens of thousands during June, and features a full line-up of large outdoor concerts, a River Giants parade, hot air balloons, and a carnival family atmosphere.

At left: The Anderson Ranch Reservoir, a popular fishing and watersport area in Southwest Idaho. Below: Night skiing at Bogus Basin Ski Resort, just outside Boise.

*B*oise uptown:
Above: Capitol Boulevard at night. Below: The new Grove Hotel and Bank of America Center—a prime concert, sports, and entertainment venue that seats 5,000 spectators and is home to the WCHL Idaho Steelheads, Boise's pro ice hockey team. At left: The scenic Boise foothills are a fitting backdrop for the city's seasonal Shakespeare Festival series.

Outside Magazine named Boise as one of the top 10 American cities in which to live.

Boise is recognized for its quality of life and economic growth. Technology giants Micron and Hewlett Packard operate key plants in the area and HP sponsors one of cycling's top yearly events — The HP Womens' Challenge. Below: The contemporary Wells Fargo Financial building is a striking addition to the capitol city skyline.

At left: Pro baseball action, Hawks Stadium. Boise hosts a pro team in the California Angels system, the Boise Hawks.

Boise is home to Boise State University and the WAC Broncos. Boise's stadium is famous for its Bronco-blue artificial turf. At right: The Humanitarian Bowl, played at BSU each December, was the setting for the contest between the University of Idaho Vandals (in black and gold) and Southern Mississippi. Former NFL great and Idaho resident, Jerry Kramer, presides over the coin toss.

Football Photos: Steve Bly, Top and right : Ed Guthero

34

Below left: Boise's professional hockey team, the Idaho Steelheads of the West Coast Hockey League, have become fan favorites at the Bank of America Center. Here the Steelheads goalie thwarts a drive. Below right: The Treasure Valley boasts two of the country's most respected and top-rated professional rodeos. The Snake River Stampede has long been a fixture in Nampa and draws thousands annually. The Caldwell Night Rodeo is one of the top events on the pro circuit. Shown here: bronc riding action at the Caldwell Night Rodeo.

Photos: Ed Guthero, Left: c/o Idaho Steelheads

At right: Shelly Williams, a recent Miss Rodeo America, from Kuna, Idaho. Shelly was named Miss Rodeo Idaho before winning the national title and is a skilled barrel racer as well. Along with Texas, Idaho cowgirls have won the most Miss Rodeo America titles over the years.

SOUTH CENTRAL
Idaho

**From the eerie landscape of the City of Rocks
to the awesome majesty of Shoshone Falls,
the South Central area of Idaho is replete
with the mysteries of nature.**

". . . a lot of state that I didn't know about . . . this Idaho."
—Ernest Hemingway

Shoshone Falls

The Snake River echoes with the thundering crash of Shoshone Falls, the "Niagara of the West." Whitewater plunges over 212 feet—a full 52 feet further than Niagara—bathing the area in a cool rainbow mist.

Thousand Springs

Cascading from a cliff wall above the Snake River near Hagerman are numerous springs believed to be the reappearance of the Lost River, which curiously sinks into a lava field near Arco—90 miles away. The Hagerman Valley is also known for its fish hatcheries and fossil beds.

Malad Gorge

The Malad Gorge is a 250 foot abyss that pours into the churning waters of the Devil's Washbowl. The Malad River then winds its way through a narrow chasm for two miles before joining the Snake River.

Twin Falls

No matter the interest, you'll find it in Twin Falls. A thriving community that offers the best features of any city, it also serves as a gateway to a wide variety of recreational and scenic opportunities—such as nearby Shoshone Falls.

City of Rocks

The strange landscape of the City of Rocks National Reserve clocks in at about 2 billion years old—making it some of the oldest rock known in the West. The sight of graffiti penned by Oregon Trail pioneers juxtaposed with professional mountain climbers looking for a new challenge just adds to the otherworldly quality.

Opposite page: Sunrise at the City of Rocks. At left: Looking over Boad Canyon in the Pioneer Mountain Range. Above: The power of Shoshone Falls.

Photos: Mark Lisk, Left: Kirk Keough

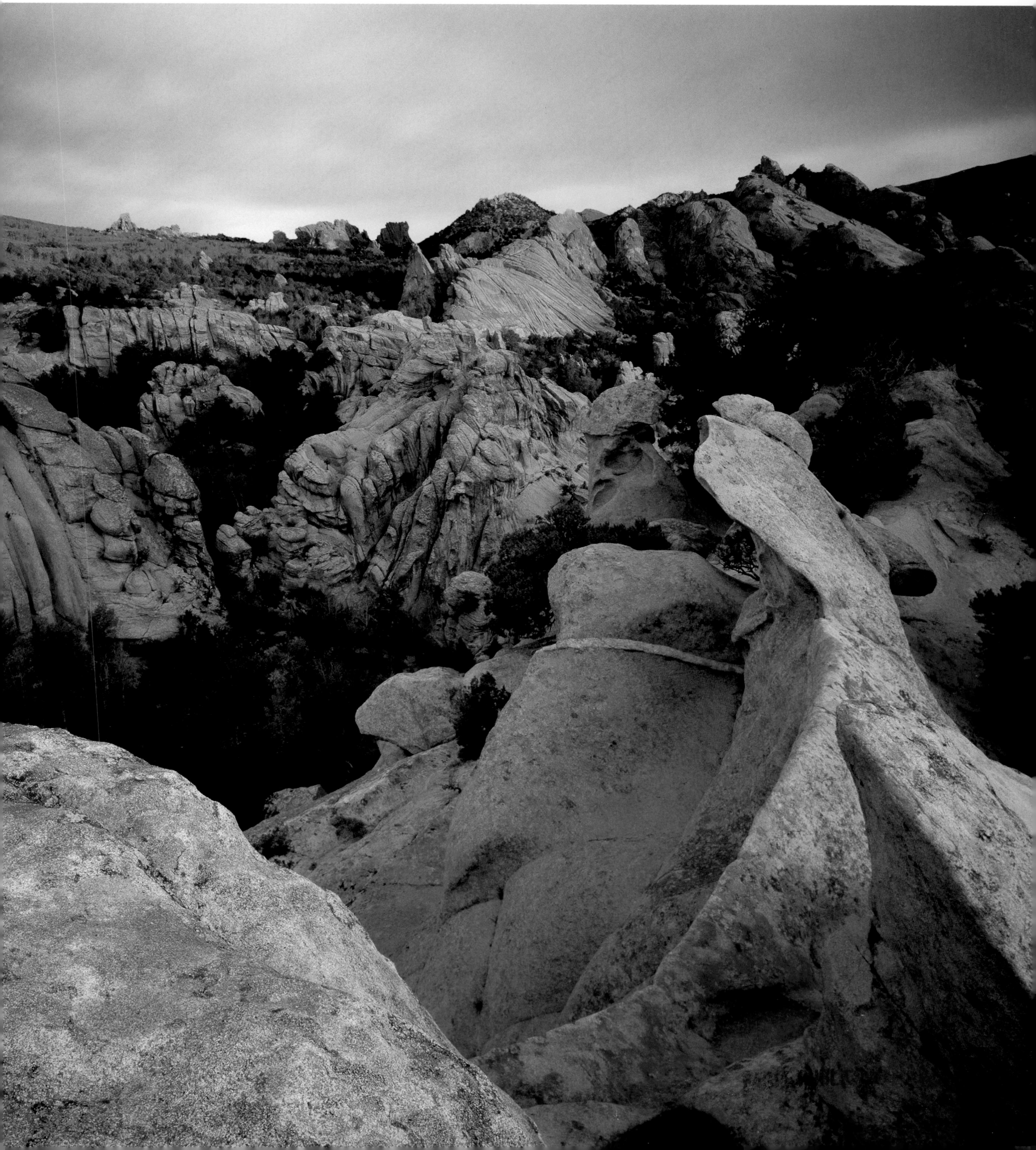

The majesty of Shoshone Falls
Photo: Stan Sinclair

At right: There is majesty in the details: A Syringa blossom, Idaho's state flower, basks in the summer sunlight. Below: A cluster of Indian paintbrush in a blaze of brilliant red.

Photos: John Baker, this spread. Previous spread: Stan Sinclair

Above: An alert coyote pauses in a golden field of dry grass. At right: Close-up on a dragonfly and his landing pad of green.

CENTRAL
Idaho

Expect mountains when you come to Idaho. With over 80 recognized ranges, Idaho is considered the most mountainous of all the Rocky Mountain States. In Central Idaho, the peaks of the Boulders, the White Clouds and the Sawtooths dominate the skies for 60 miles in each direction.

"I like Idaho. The crystal streams. The rushing rivers. The forest. The mountains. The lakes as blue as paint. The splash of mountain ash or maple. The foam of the Syringa, the state's official flower. The awesome wastes. The fruitful fields. The warm friendliness of crossroads and town. The high sky over all." —A.B. Guthrie, author of Big Sky

Sun Valley

Sun Valley is the very definition of the American winter vacation. The nation's first destination ski resort, Sun Valley boasts a world-class mountain with a quality ski school and experienced instructors. Apres-ski, tourists and residents enjoy a rich variety of activities.

Sawtooth Mountains

The untamed Sawtooth Mountains are the crown jewels of Idaho's mountain ranges, and stretch 30 miles long and 15 miles wide. The headwaters of the Salmon River originate here, feeding over 300 alpine lakes nestled between the jagged peaks.

The rugged majesty of Central Idaho's Sawtooth national recreation area. At right: The jagged peaks of the Sawtooth Mountains loom above a log jam on the Snake River. Photos: Steve Bly

Salmon River

The Salmon River is one of Idaho's most defining landmarks, with abundant fishing, whitewater rafting and kayaking. An impressive 420 miles long, the Salmon is also one of the longest undammed rivers in the continental U.S and nick-named the "River of No Return" due to its difficult passage.

Galena Summit

There is a spectacular vista of the entire Sawtooth Range from Galena Summit.

Salmon

The old mining town of Salmon is named for the fish that makes its annual journey from the Pacific Ocean to inland rivers in the summer and fall. Today, Salmon is the gateway to some of the last wild river systems in the country, making it a popular tourist destination for whitewater rafters and kayakers.

At left: Sapphire Lake in the White Cloud Mountain Range.
Below: Frosted reeds on Fourth of July Lake.

Photos: Mark Lisk

Idaho is people in motion on a landscape built for solitude or speed.

A portfolio of Idaho recreational images by photographer Steve Bly.

*S*un Valley, Idaho is a skier's dream.
Famous as the country's first destination
ski resort, Sun Valley has long defined the
classic winter vacation. This Central
Idaho gem features 78 ski runs. Nestled
in its mountain haven, it is truly a
winter wonderland.

Classic Sun Valley defines the skier's dream.

Photos: Steve Bly, Top: Kirk Keough

Top: Mountain bluebells adorn the banks of the Middle Fork of the Salmon River at Pistol Creek Rapid. Above: Early morning frost on the edge of Toxaway Lake.

*S*now dusts the banks of the Middle Fork of the Salmon
River near Boundary Creek. At right: Frost covered wildflowers at dawn in the Sawtooth Mountains.

Opposite left: Looking over Broad Canyon in the Pioneer Mountain Range. At left: Catch of the day for a steelhead fisherman and his wife on the Main Salmon River. Below: River rocks in the Middle Fork of the Salmon River near Jackass Creek. Bottom: Lichen covered rocks on the ridgelines of the White Cloud Peaks.

Photos: Mark Lisk

Rafters soaking in a natural spring on the Salmon River. Below left: A group of rams walk through a dry meadow near the banks of the Main Salmon River. Below: Four Lakes Basin in the White Cloud Range, Sawtooth National Forest.

Photos: Mark Lisk

Above: In a dreamlike scene, snow fills the barren landscape of Craters of the Moon National Monument.
Below: An ancient white pine in the White Cloud Range makes a striking image despite the ravages of time.

Opposite top: Water rushes past an autumn fisherman on the banks of the Salmon River.
Opposite bottom: Camp tents glow in the twilight as travellers rest during a trip up the Salmon River.
Below: A glowing wall tent in the Lost River Range is a striking image of mountain solitude.

Photos: Mark Lisk

Photos: John Baker, Steve Bly, Kirk Keough , Opposite page: Mark Lisk

At left and bottom right: There is beauty in the quiet places. Even in solitude Idaho whispers its grandeur. A lone horse and a weather-beaten shack near the foot of Mt. Borah. Bottom left: A view of Stanley on the Salmon River with the mighty Sawtooth Mountains stretching across the horizon. Below: Llama-packing near Sun Valley. Opposite right: At Silver Creek a flyfisherman casts against vivid Autumn colors. Silver Creek was a favorite fishing spot of the great writer Ernest Hemingway.

A potpourri of recreational activities from throughout the state.

cut loose

Photos by Tim Brown except boat & snowmobile by John Baker

*Horse-packing on the
Lost River Range.*

Photo: Mark Lisk

65

A radiant view of sunlight reflecting off the mountains at Trail Creek.

The great Teton Mountains loom in the distance, as viewed from the Idaho side of the Idaho/ Wyoming border at Reece Homestead in Eastern Idaho.

At right: The restored Liberty Theatre in Hailey, Central Idaho.

Photos: At top- Steve Bly, G. Yascot, Fish Creek Enterprises (barn)

Colorful traditional dress images from an Idaho centennial gathering of Native American tribes. Participants include the Shoshone-Bannock, Nez Perce, Kootenai, Coeur d'Alene, Kalispel, and Northern Paiute tribes from Idaho as well as visiting groups from Canada and neighboring states.

Native American culture is beautifully displayed at the Fort Hall Shoshone Bannock Tribal Museum, as well as the Idaho Museum of Natural History at Idaho State University in Pocatello.

Photos: Ed Gubrero

EASTERN
Idaho

Eastern

In Eastern Idaho, the snowcapped peaks of the Grand Tetons feed thundering waterfalls, glistening lakes and free flowing rivers. As a neighbor to Yellowstone and Teton National Parks, it shares much of the same spectacular beauty and awesome adventure...but without the crowds. "Is there contentment beyond the confines of urban living? You bet. In Idaho. God has carved out a special preview of the hereafter for those who prefer life in a natural state."
—Andrew Harper, Editor of *The Hideaway Report*

Harriman State Park

Harriman State Park, formerly known as the Railroad Ranch, was the summer playground of Union Pacific owners Roland and Averell Harriman (who also created Sun Valley). Wildlife abounds at the park with elk, moose, beaver, muskrats, bald eagles, osprey, trumpeter swans and other waterfowl.

Bear Lake

This 120-square-mile lake straddles the Idaho-Utah border and is known for its brilliant turquoise waters, caused by limestone particles. The color is most spectacular when viewed from the Highway 89 summit.

Rexburg

Nestled in the scenic Upper Snake River Valley, Rexburg is listed as one of the top 100 small towns in America. Great boating, camping, fishing and cultural events abound.

Lava Hot Springs

For centuries, Indian tribes gathered at these natural hot water springs, calling them the healing waters. Geologists theorize that the water has been a consistent 110 degrees for at least 50 million years. Large hot pools abound, making this a popular destination.

Grand Targhee Resort

Nestled on the sunny west side of the Grand Tetons, Grand Targhee Ski and Summer Resort enjoys uncrowded slopes, abundant powder (more than 500 inches annually) and awesome Teton scenery. National ski magazines rate Grand Targhee among the top five resorts in the west for snow quality and quantity.

Pocatello

With 45,000 residents, Pocatello is Idaho's second largest city. The town was originally the administrative center of the Union Pacific Railroad. Today, it offers skiing, snowmobiling, an extensive park system and a vast array of fishing and hunting opportunities.

Henry's Fork

The Henry's Fork of the Snake River is known as one of the finest dry fly streams in the country. It is known best for its smooth currents, prolific insect hatches, and large, though selective, trout. It is over sixty miles long, and there's a stretch for everyone, beginners and experts alike.

Idaho Falls

A gateway for fly-fishing and snowmobilers, Idaho Falls is also a launching pad to Yellowstone National Park and the Idaho National Engineering Laboratory. Originally named Eagle Rock, the town founders built a weir to attract more settlers and changed its name accordingly. It worked. Today, it's Idaho's third largest city.

Driggs

This foothills town offers a breathtaking view of the west side of the Tetons.

At right: The mist rises on Henry's Fork on the Snake River against a backdrop of the Teton Mountains. Below: Sunlight casts a golden aura on a classic old Idaho barn. Opposite left: Lightning flashes above the amber waves of an Idaho wheat field.

Photos: Steve Bly

At right: A rustic barn near Driggs, Idaho.
Below: "Catch and release" rainbow trout on
the South Fork of the Snake River.
Opposite top: The South Fork of the Snake
River in Eastern Idaho. Opposite bottom:
Henry's Fork of the Snake River below
Upper Mesa / Targee.

Mesa Falls, near Henry's Fork in autumn.
Photo: Glenn Oakley

Unique
Idaho Resorts

Deluxe skiing at Sun Valley's Bald Mountain

Unique
Idaho Golf Courses

*The renowned Coeur d'Alene Resort
Golf Course from the 13th tee*

Sun Valley®

There is no other place with quite the magic and energy of Sun Valley, the original American winter resort. Since 1936 Sun Valley has defined the classic winter vacation and remains recognized as the country's top destination ski resort. Readers of the respected *Conde Nast Traveler Magazine* named Sun Valley Resort as "one of the best in the world."

The rugged beauty and warmth of Sun Valley's spectacular day lodges (such as the River Run Plaza shown at right), the stately views of the Wood River Valley, the Sawtooth and Pioneer Mountains, the world-class skating shows at Sun Valley Lodge, numerous boutiques and shops as well as exquisite cuisine all combine to create the Sun Valley mystique.

Sun Valley is an all-season resort, but its skiing is legendary. Dollar Mountain and Bald Mountain are ski havens and the area boasts 78 seemingly endless ski runs.

For individual vacations or business retreats, Sun Valley has a special magic all its own.

Photo: Paul Dalzell

• *For more information contact: 1-800-786-8259 www.sunvalley.com*

The Coeur d'Alene

COEUR d'ALENE, IDAHO

The Coeur d'Alene has tamed the Northwest wilderness with luxurious accommodations and five-star amenities on the shores of one of the world's most scenic lakes. The resort's restaurants offer an exceptional menu of dining options, from Italian to Northwest classics in three waterfront facilities including Beverly's, winner of the prestigious DiRoNa Fine Dining Award and Grand Award from *The Wine Spectator.* The resort's golf course has received a Gold Medal from *Golf* magazine and a five-star rating from *Golf Digest,* the highest rating in the industry. Guests also enjoy the full-service Euro spa, cruises on Lake Coeur d'Alene, shopping in the Resort Plaza, strolls on the boardwalk, and relaxing in one of the resort's 371 lakeside rooms. Located just 40 minutes from Spokane, Washington, International Airport.

• *Reservations can be made by calling 800.688.5253 or 208.765.4000, or at www.cdaresort.com.*

The city of Coeur d' Alene has earned the designation "All-America City" from the National Civic League. For skiers, Coeur d'Alene is in close proximity to ski havens Silver Mountain and Schweitzer Mountain. Coeur d' Alene is truly a four season destination for fun.

The Lodge at
Riggins Hot Springs

*I*daho's Salmon River Canyon is the setting for this secluded mountain resort featuring a natural hot springs spa, invigorating mountain air, delicious gourmet dining, a stocked trout pond, and bounded by miles of spectacular forests. Surrounded by serene wilderness, the Lodge provides an ideal setting for business getaways, weddings, and family reunions.

The spectacular Salmon River beckons and the unspoiled river canyon is an outdoor playground or place of solace. Renowned for its homestyle atmosphere, the lodge's generous bedrooms are designed for comfort in a style reminiscent of the Native Americans who first discovered the Springs.

If your business associates or board of directors need a chance to get away, work, and then relax together, there is a fully equipped Conference Center available for your retreat. The Lodge at Riggins Hot Springs is a mountain gem that awaits you.

The LODGE
At Riggins Hot Springs

• *For more information contact:*
The Lodge at Riggins Hot Springs,
P.O. Box 1247, Riggins, Idaho
83549, (208) 628-3785,
www.rhslodge.com

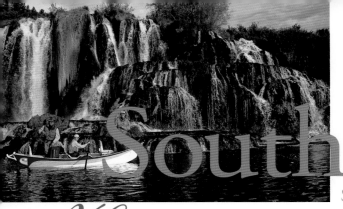

South Fork Lodge
SWAN VALLEY, IDAHO

*H*idden on a secluded stretch of the mighty Snake River, South Fork Lodge is a rustic blend of Western lodging and beautiful natural surroundings that is considered one of the premier fly-fishing retreats in the country. The river is a wonderful year-round, dry-fly destination while the region is distinguished by river canyons and a rolling agricultural landscape abutting the foothills of the Grand Teton Mountains. The natural wonders of Idaho, Wyoming, Yellowstone, and Montana are all easily accessible. The nearby Snake River Canyon hosts the largest winter roost of bald eagles in the continental U.S.

South Fork Lodge is the vision of Mark Rockefeller, an angler and sportsman dedicated to preserving this magnificent area as a natural recreation resource for years to come. South Fork Lodge, with its uniquely designed main lodge, spacious accommodations, extensive fly shop, outfitting and guide services, and an exclusive restaurant overlooking breathtaking waters will rival any retreat you've ever seen on the banks of a great river. South Fork Lodge is an all-season facility and two of the country's leading ski resorts (Grand Targee and Jackson Hole) are located just an hour from the lodge. South Fork Lodge also boasts a sizable, private Nordic Ski Center where guests can enjoy abundant scenery and wildlife. The well-equipped lodge is also an ideal setting for intimate business retreats and corporate groups. No matter what the saeason, South Fork Lodge has something for everyone.

•*For more information contact: P.O. Box 22, Swan Valley, ID 83449* • *Toll-free: 1-877-347-4735* • *www.southforklodge.com*

UNIQUE Golf Courses

McCALL

McCall Golf Course

Hayden Lake Country Club

HAYDEN LAKE

TWIN FALLS

Blue Lakes Country Club

Sun Valley Golf Course

SUN VALLEY

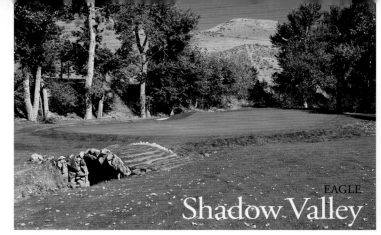
EAGLE
Shadow Valley

IDAHO FALLS
Pine Crest

BOISE
Crane Creek Country Club

BOISE
Hillcrest Country Club

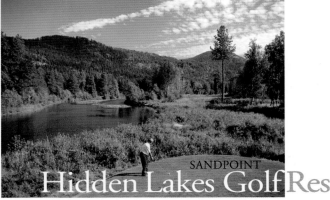
SANDPOINT
Hidden Lakes Golf Resort

COEUR d'ALENE
Coeur d'Alene Resort Golf Course

UNIQUE
Idaho

A COLLECTION OF IDAHO'S MOST

- The Hagadone House
- The House at Robie Springs
- The Central Idaho
    Guest House
- The Moore House
- The House at Eagle Creek
- The Sabala Cabin

- The Vermilion House
- The Handy House
- The Healy Tree House
- The Couch House
- The Cloninger House
- The Stoecklein Ranch
    (Bar Horseshoe Ranch)

HOMES

ORIGINAL AND DISTINCTIVE HOMES

The Hagadone House

C O E U R   D ' A L E N E ,   I D A H O

Photography by Quicksilver Studios

Overlooking Lake Coeur d'Alene in North Idaho, this internationally styled Hagadone home was designed to incorporate materials from around the globe. There is a great use of exotic woods including: Mahogany Chenille, Bubinga Wood and quartered African Satinwood, Sycamore and Santos. The woods are combined in harmonious patterns and are accented by the stonework created with materials imported from Italy, France, Germany, South America and Asia. The home occupies a 16-acre site on Stanley Hill above the city of Coeur d'Alene, and the complex consists of approximately 30,000 square feet. It also includes an adjacent indoor

ARCHITECT: WARREN SHEETS • BUILDER: PANCO CONSTRUCTION

tennis court (which can be converted to a banquet facility for up to 550 guests), a driving range with putting green, an 11-car garage and caretaker facilities. The home features 10 fireplaces, 17 bathrooms, indoor and outdoor tennis courts and swimming pools, a complete recreation center with a fully-automated bowling alley, and extensive waterscape features such as serenity pools, waterfalls and fountains.

Multiple views of the Hagadone House: (Opposite, clockwise from top) Aerial views; exterior at dusk; living room; dining room; pool at night. (Clockwise from top left) Bar, library, kitchen, bathroom. Warren Sheets Design of San Francisco fashioned the interior, which transforms raw space into sensual art.

The House at
Robie Springs

Architect Dennis Stevens: A Legacy and the Land

J ROBIE SPRINGS, IDAHO

ust half an hour from downtown Boise, amid the rugged mountains of Idaho's Robie Creek, a master architect is quietly fulfilling a vision . . . 15 homes covering 50 acres.

Dennis Stephens, a direct disciple of legendary architect Frank Lloyd Wright, is designing all the homes to be part of the environment. The community will have no fences and no visible boundaries. It will be an example of modern habitation harmoniously integrated with a natural wilderness landscape.

This remarkable two-level, 5,000 square-foot home grows out of the hill and follows the land's natural slope while offering multiple breathtaking views. Even indoors there is no sense of enclosure, just interaction between nature and home.

The materials, tones, and textures of the inside of the home reflect the natural elements and visual lines outside of it. "Living in a concept," Stevens calls it. "If it looks like it's been here for 50 years, I've done my job."

Though the structure is anchored 12 feet into granite with 650 anchor bolts, the house floats freely, creating a feeling of movement and reinforcing the symbolic interaction with its surroundings.

ARCHITECT: DENNIS STEVENS - ROBIE SPRINGS, ID
BUILDER: ARCHITECTURAL ENTERPRISES, LTD - ROBIE SPRINGS, ID

Photography by Phil McClain

*R*obie Springs is an opportunity to show the world that homes and nature can exist harmoniously when approached with a conscientious design and respect for the land. Before beginning the Robie Springs project, Architect Stevens and his wife, Jackie, undertook a three-year search—considering Colorado, New Mexico, and Arizona before falling in love with Idaho's Robie Creek region.

The various elements and room blend, overlap, integrate, and weave wonderfully throughout both floors in this clean, contemporary design.

At age 17, Robie Springs architect Dennis Stevens was one of legendary architect Frank Lloyd Wright's youngest apprentices. Stevens lived and worked with Wright over a period of five years.

Photography by Tim Brown

K E T C H U M , I D A H O

This guesthouse offers airy comfort to an extended family with its unique "W" shape and ample floorplan that includes a great room, two master bedroom suites, dining room, playroom, bunkroom, bar, study and kitchen. Horizontal windows, siding and stone veneer patterns are compatible with the flat site. A highlight is the roof deck area that provides comfortable outdoor space with a fireplace, hot tub, barbecue and bar access, and seating areas with spectacular views of the mountains and ski area.

ARCHITECT: McMILLEN PYNN ARCHITECTURE - KETCHUM, ID
BUILDER: UPHAM CONSTRUCTION - HAILEY, ID

The Central Idaho
Guest
House

The main entry comprises two large center-pivoting glass panels that create a transparent corner at the center. The interiors have a natural, modern appearance with natural stone and clear maple wood flooring, and accent walls in vivid primary colors. A unique feature of this house is the roof which doubles as an entertainment area (top, opposite page).

This table was designed by the home's architect, Mark Pynn, AIA

The Moore House

COEUR D'ALENE, IDAHO

Photography by Quicksilver Studios

The Moore House on Lake Coeur d'Alene sits at the very tip of Arrow Point on a basalt rock outcropping. Built in 1970 as a summer cottage, the house has been remodeled to emphasize the view and enhance its spaciousness. The 2,000 square foot house is finished with a pale grey interior to show off the natural blues and greens of the lake that surrounds on three sides. The furnishings are low profile and accented by a collection of nude sculptures in black and white.

ARCHITECT: ELMER JORDAN -
COEUR D' ALENE, ID
BUILDER: ALLAN EBORALL -
COEUR D' ALENE, ID

Above left: A round port-hole-like window was added in the loft. Above right: The remodeled bathroom features a steam bath with a lake view.

*C*lean, contempo-
rary lines are
evident through-
out all levels of
the house on the
lake, both in the
interior structural
design and the
stylish furnishings
shown on these
pages.

The House at
Eagle Creek
"Form Follows Landscape"

The House at Eagle Creek

Opposite page: The copper clad glass pyramids create a striking silhouette on the approach to the residence. At left: The birch walls and ceilings in the living, dining and kitchen areas maximize the effects of light.

KETCHUM, IDAHO

Photography by Tim Brown & Fred Lindholm

This geometrically complex home on Eagle Creek Road north of Ketchum is an unusual creation among the sagebrush hills. The architect's objective was to lift the human spirit, and the expression of that desire is most notable in the five plaster and glass-capped pyramids that rise up from the rooftop. From the exterior, the pyramids create their own ridge of mountaintops, which is suited to the geography of the Eagle Creek area. The glass tops create a wonderful experience of light and reflection once inside. Each pyramid rises out of a different section of the home, giving the sense of a ceiling plan rather than floor plan. The largest pyramid rises over the living area, and the nearest two shed light on the dining and kitchen areas. The fourth and fifth provide a lighted intimacy to bedrooms.

ARCHITECT : JACK SMITH, FAIA - KETCHUM, ID
BUILDER : INTERMOUNTAIN CONSTRUCTION -
IDAHO FALLS, ID - JEFF OGDEN

*M*ultiple views of the house at Eagle Creek
demonstrate how it re-interprets the landscape
to become its own mountain reflection.

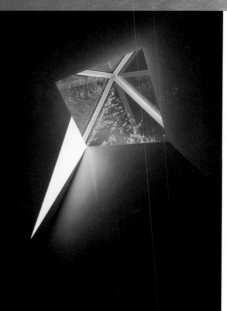

Top: The chimneys, which are poured-in-place concrete, ground the home and balance the soaring pyramids.

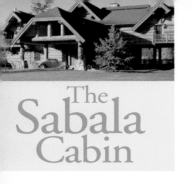

The Sabala Cabin

Garland Log Homes of Montana cut and tapered the milled logs to give them a handcrafted look.

McCALL, IDAHO

Photography by Roger Wade

The Sabala Cabin is located on a plateau above the Payette River overlooking a wilderness area. The covered deck over the master suite capitalizes on the mountain and river views and extends the usable outdoor areas. The interior design emotes a rustic elegance with an English country motif. Built in 1996, most of the home's 4,100 square feet are located in the central great room. The great room has a 33-foot ceiling and opens to the kitchen and dining room. Lofty windows enhance the height of this area and offer views of the river and surrounding wetlands. A seven foot chandelier graces the room, while cherry bookshelves and a marble fireplace add warmth to the study. The master bedroom's interior finish shows a French influence that creates a comfortable elegance. The bold mix of colorful fabrics and wall-coverings and a crushed marble fireplace add warmth. This room has two private decks that face the river and the front of the house.

ARCHITECT: KEVIN McKEE - BOISE, ID
BUILDER: SCOTT HEDRICK CONSTRUCTION - BOISE, ID

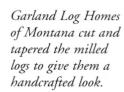

The
Sabala
Cabin

An upper-level catwalk overlooks the great room and links the guest wing with the master bedroom.

The open kitchen presents views to the other rooms.
Large interior logs carved into a tall archway frame the
modern appliances and ample counter space. A
fireplace brings the hearth into the kitchen with a solid
oak mantel from a pre-Civil War barn.

The Vermilion House

EAGLE, IDAHO

Photography by Lisa Brown

The Vermilion House occupies five acres in Eagle, offering a 360-degree view of Boise city lights, foothills, and mountains. Several different architectural attributes are melded together to create the overall effect. The exterior walls climb in an outward slope and the five-and-a-half foot overhangs add a nice horizontal touch. Functional aerial planters decorate the front entryway and the eighteen foot cantilevered rear deck. Floating triangular roofs project out between the planters, tying the sloping roofs to the flats.

The interior of the home benefits from the high glass that allows light to play off the walls, angles and architectural projections. Lower windows, which are set back one foot into the walls, offer inspiring views.

ARCHITECT & BUILDER:
SCOTT SNYDER DESIGN - BOISE, ID

Above: and left: A floor mosaic in Turkish marble and Italian black granite graces the front entry, giving off warmth and complementing the angular glass of the entry door. Greenery in the planters overhead add a touch of the outdoors.

Above: Grey slate walls and floors in the master bath are set off by stainless steel accents. Right: The kitchen's clear wood finish accents the asymmetrical black granite countertops. Outwardly angled cabinetry add to the theme of simplicity and a red vegetable sink adds a point of interest to the kitchen area.

*H*igh porthole windows send
light shimmering off the stainless
steel fireplace, and shadows
animate the white background
in this spacious area.

The Handy House

K E T C H U M ,   I D A H O

Photography   by   Tim   Brown

The Handy Residence and Guesthouse in Sun Valley harmonize with the natural environment of gently rolling hills that display native grasses and high desert sagebrush. Built entirely of natural materials with clear finishes to enhance their inherent beauty, the house was designed with a central "spine" with rooms projecting off each side to maximize the spectacular views. Warm tones, clean lines, and modern sculptures are features of this beautiful contemporary home.

ARCHITECT: MARK PYNN AIA, McMILLEN PYNN ARCHITECTS - KETCHUM, ID
BUILDER: ENGELMANN CONSTRUCTION - KETCHUM, ID

The natural beauty of Idaho quartzite stone, birch, and fir woods are illuminated with indirect light.

Guests enjoy outdoor gatherings on the patio with a spectacular view of Bald Mountain.

The Guesthouse was carefully sited and designed to reflect the main house, blend into its natural site while taking advantage of the views; and to respect the views and the privacy of the main house.

Exterior sculptures accent the architect's intent of linear and modular appearance.

Casual elegance is the theme for entertaining in the rich warmth of the dining area.

The Healy Tree House

S A N D P O I N T , I D A H O

The Healy Tree House is "livable art" perched high in the branches of three massive trees on Lake Pend Oreille near Sandpoint. The tree house was conceived of, and built by Jim and Deanne Healy to inspire childlike awe at the wonders of nature. From the entrance stairway that swings into the tree limbs on a sandbag counterbalance, to the lookout tower forty-seven feet above the ground, this nest of a house invites its guests to revel in whimsy.

ARCHITECT & BUILDER:
    JIM & DEANNE HEALY - SANDPOINT, ID

Photography by Quicksilver Studios

Inspired by the architect Gaudi of Spain, the soft curves of the only new windows in the house merge the room subtly with the panorama.

An African fertility pole and hand-hewn plank staircase extended by boat ladders provide an invitation to the upper levels.

The king bed in the second-level nook provides luxurious lake views, while the third level entertains those younger at heart with stargazing and wildlife viewings.

The living room, kitchen and bathroom are located on the first level. Antique leaded windows from England, portholes and memorabilia from Valentino's yacht, a bathroom wrapped with copper walls, and natural slate floors highlight the living spaces.

The Couch House

Photography by Lisa Brown

Robert L. Couch, a native Idahoan, designed and built this spectacular log home. Bob loved the outdoors and brought its feel indoors with massive, hand-peeled Ponderosa Pine logs from Lowman, Idaho. This home sits on a one acre rim with awesome views of Squaw Butte, Bogus Basin, and Spur Wing Country Club Golf Course. The open loft area overlooks the great room and formal living room with captivating views out the west and east windows.

The kitchen cabinets and floor, as well as all doors of this home, are solid hickory and the countertops are slab granite. The front door is made from hand-cut glass and features a mountain stream motif, while the entry is slate—again bringing the textures of nature indoors (see p. 125).

As shown on the following page, the home's spacious master bedroom is complete with its own fireplace constructed of stucco and inlaid with tumbled marble.

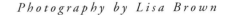

ARCHITECT & BUILDER: BOB COUCH - EAGLE, ID

ob enjoyed entertaining and playing pool in the lower level game room, complete with bar, refridgerator, ice-maker and dishwasher. Also shown here are the living room and master bedroom, both featuring fireplaces.

Above: Double glass and hickory French doors lead into the master bath. Tumbled marble completes the bathroom countertops. The room has 12-inch tile flooring, shower, and jacuzzi tub. Also shown (at right) are the stunning cut glass entry door and (at top) the spacious kitchen area.

The Cloninger House

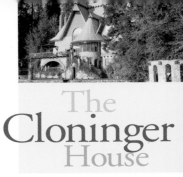

COEUR D'ALENE, IDAHO

Photography by Quicksilver Studios

This unique home brings extra magic to a summer cruise along the shores of Northern Idaho's Lake Coeur d'Alene. The trees at maximum foliage, air vibrant with blossoming flowers, and water shimmering with morning's soft light create the backdrop for Cloninger's stately, charming stone cottage that beckons guests ashore. Dubbed "Toad Hall," from *The Wind in the Willows,* this finely crafted blend of steel, concrete, stone, Northwest pine, fir, alder, and cedar seems to whisper, "Come inside and explore."

ARCHITECT & BUILDER: GLEN CLONINGER · SPOKANE, WA

*G*len and Pam Cloninger wanted a lake cabin possessing historic flavor and this home with its unique design featuring a witch-hat roof top, turrets, stone archways, twisting brick chimneys, coffered ceilings, and window seats, charmingly epitomizes their goal.

* Spread information source:
Coeur d'Alene Magazine,
Summer 2001

The clever design makes the home appear more spacious than the actual square footage, while projecting a much larger feeling due to the roof's steep expanse. At 60 degrees, this roof is the steepest pitch architect Cloninger has ever designed.

This unique house was a construction challenge, having wood beams embedded in stone and staircases buried in bedrock. Master stone masons George Sherman and Johnny Fry built the walls of Idaho granite.

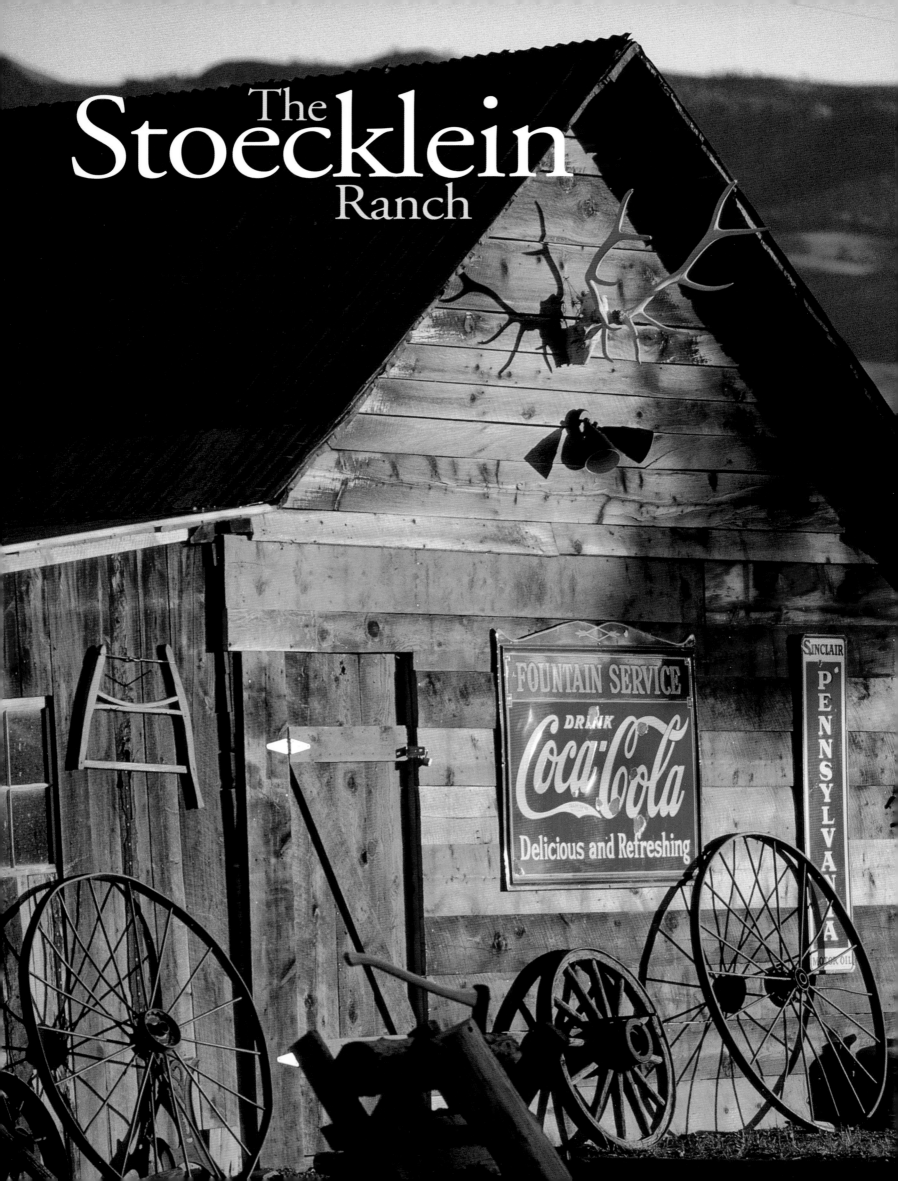

The Stoecklein
Ranch

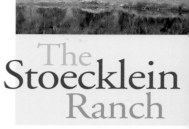
Photography by David Stoecklein

MACKAY, IDAHO

"We built the main house and guest cabins in 1990," says renowned photographer David Stoecklein. "We tried to use as many materials from the original building on the ranch as possible. The main home is constructed from six old cabins dating back to the 1880s. The barn, guest houses, and workshop were all refurbished using old materials."

The ranch is a family retreat and photo location for David's work and it's a working cattle and hay ranch. "The Big Lost Valley is one of the most spectacular valleys in the U.S. and that is why we chose to have our family ranch here," says Stoecklein.

OWNER: DAVID WALTER STOECKLEIN - MACKAY, ID
also known as the Bar Horseshoe Ranch

Multiple views of the Bar Horseshoe Ranch: At right: Cowboy regalia hangs by the front porch. Bottom: The bunkhouse set up for a photograph in one of Stoeklein's western books. Below: Mounted buffalo hangs over the bar.

Above: Old sheep camp set up in a meadow under Mt. Borah, the highest peak in Idaho. At right: Warm Spring Creek runs through the Stoeklein Ranch.

133

Clockwise beginning top left: The bar at the main house; a rustic door with ranch branding marks; one of two master bedrooms at the ranch; a windmill used in many of David's photos.

The house is furnished
with Western antiques.

The ranch breathes Western heritage in its essence and details.

*S*toecklein
Ranch is also an
actual working
ranch. At right:
The rustic
kitchen and
dining area.

The Ellis House

Photography by Tim Brown

The Ellis House is a chic modernist home situated on the aspen and spruce tree acreage of Golden Eagle Ranch in the Sun Valley area. The main vista for the home is the historic Union Pacific Railway Bridge, an arched trussed creation that spans the Big Wood River and inspired the design of the Ellis home. The architect incorporated the trussed bridge curvature by including a thirty-six-foot-long, sky lit Porte-Cochere colonnade entrance. The cantilevered canopy leads visitors to the dramatic five-foot-wide pivotal rusted steel entry door. The floor-to-ceiling windows in the living room create a frame for the historic bridge view. Visible from the entryway is a double helix staircase, and a circular powder room with an elevated glass sink mounted on a curly maple sculptured pedestal. The grandiose round dining room opens in to the kitchen with ample storage in stainless steel floor-to-ceiling pull out cabinets.

ARCHITECT: EDDY SVIDGAL - KETCHUM, ID
BUILDER: FRANK BASHISTA - KETCHUM, ID

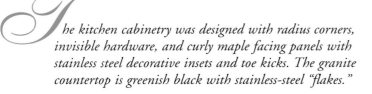 *he kitchen cabinetry was designed with radius corners, invisible hardware, and curly maple facing panels with stainless steel decorative insets and toe kicks. The granite countertop is greenish black with stainless-steel "flakes."*

The interior fabrics, carpets, and colors are predominately soft to deep golds and purples contrasted with light woods, steel, glass, aluminum and concrete. The overall effect combines a modern edginess against the color schemes of the mountainous region.

Chelonia

S U N   V A L L E Y , I D A H O

Photography by Alan Weintraub

Chelonia, designed by architect Bart Prince, is nestled on 12 acres in a valley of the mighty Sawtooths near Sun Valley. The shingled roof curves gracefully over the split-faced, honey-colored concrete, which mirrors the texture and flow of the foothills. The complex and organic exterior is held in contrast to the simple interior design. Flowing walls create pockets of space rather than formal rooms within the 3,000-square-foot home. The nucleus is the living room with a massive skylight that arches over the spacious room, bathing it in sunlight. Wings on either side of the main quarters contain the master bedroom and guest rooms. These rooms are markedly different with a warm and comforting ambiance created by the concrete walls. The main level of the home includes a dining area, formal living area with fireplace and entertainment area with built-in bronze cabinetry. The powder room and laundry

ARCHITECT: BART PRINCE - ALBEQUERQUE, NM
BUILDER: JACK MCNAMARA - SUN VALLEY, ID

room, at opposite ends of the great room, are cylindrical in shape and capped by skylights with steel points, framing the view of the sky. The bedrooms are on a slightly lower level, connected by tubular ramp hallways. The master bedroom has two decks with one off the master bath, which includes a Jacuzzi tub. The guest bedroom wing has two bedrooms—each with its own covered deck—and a bath. A large entertainment deck with a Jacuzzi and magnificent views completes the southeast side of the home.

The interior of this home challenges conventional floorplans with its arching ceilings, twisting corridors and curving walls. It is the epitome of organic structure in its ability to both challenge and blend with the landscape.

*T*he home designed by Bart Prince beneath the Sawtooths successfully highlights the contours, textures, and flow of the magnificent landscape. The home is situated on 12 acres at the intersection of three valleys. There is a creek on the north side of the home and the grounds are covered with native grasses, wildflowers, and sagebrush.

The Ketchum House

• *Materials define space* • *Angles and shapes define flow* • *Colors and textures create warmth and character.*

Opposite: Spanning the foyer and living room is the upper floor bridge. Made of obscured glass panels framed by hardwood floor planking and supported by natural steel members, the bridge flows gracefully from side to side, leading you down a matching hardwood suspended staircase. The stainless steel cable adds to the flowing pattern.

KETCHUM, IDAHO

Photography by Tim Brown

The request: "I would like a home designed with materials which create a feeling of indoor/outdoor relationships, which is comfortable and easy to live in and exudes a style of its own."

Chosen for his ability to utilize materials and space that go beyond the norm, Architect Tobin Dougherty created a home of individual character, shape, and style.

The sharp, soaring lines of the exterior are complimented by the colored cement plaster and wood siding, blending and helping to ground the building with the surrounding environment.

Amongst the concrete, steel and glass there is a warmth and comfort. The radiant, heated stained concrete floors on the lower level are warm in look and feel during the cold winter months but retain the cool for warm summer days. Many wall surfaces are integrated color plaster finish. The hardwood surfaces, cabinets, flooring, and windows also help add warmth to the interior environment.

ARCHITECT: TOBIN DOUGHERTY, TOBIN ARCHITECTS - KETCHUM, ID
BUILDER: ENGELMANN CONSTRUCTION - KETCHUM, ID

*M*ultiple views of
the Ketchum House
including the
obscured glass floor
panels, framed in
hardwood, on the
home's Upper Floor
Bridge (top).

Entry wall: All building angles converge to a floating entry wall with a pivoting door surrounded by glass and covered by a large cantilevered cover.

147

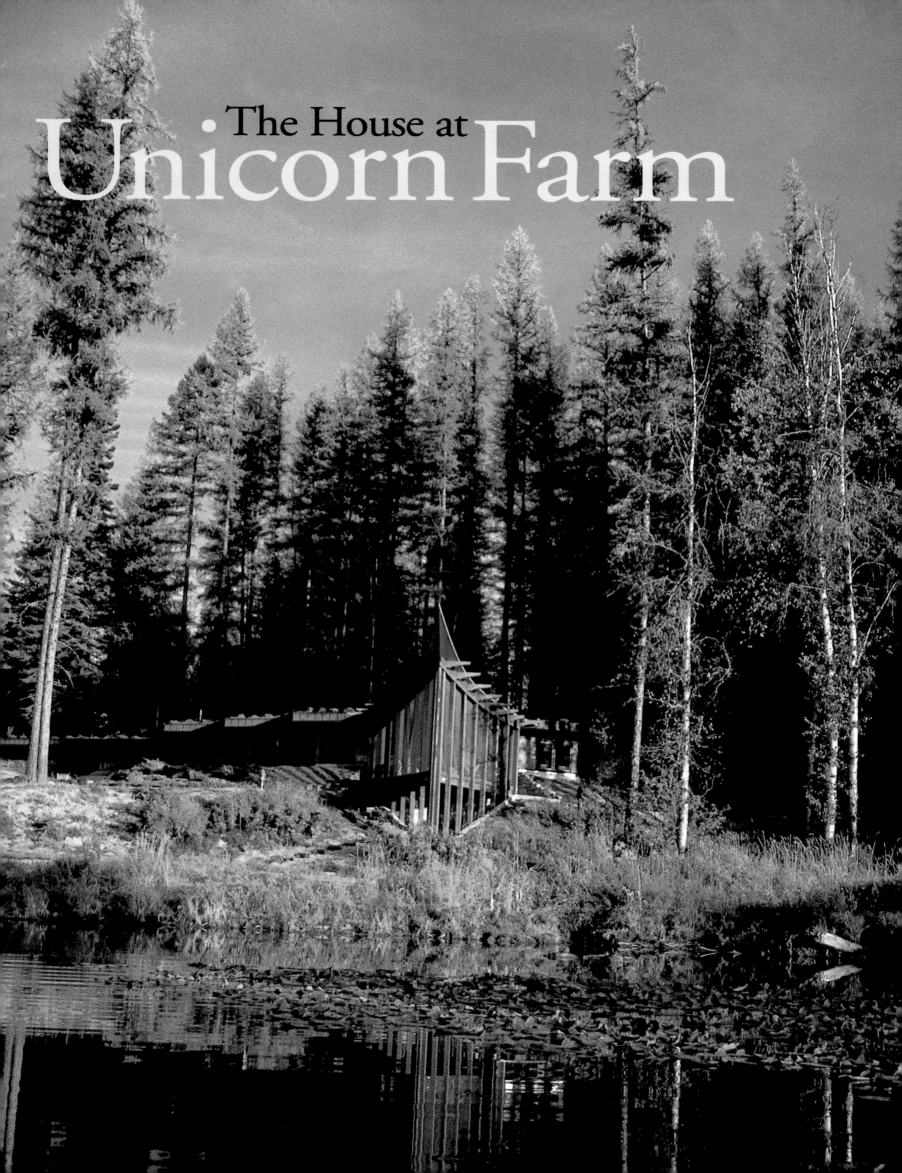

The House at
Unicorn Farm

Photography by Joseph Henry Wythe

S A N D P O I N T ,   I D A H O

*A*rchitect Joseph Henry Wythe built *Unicorn Farm* in a "magical part of the forest, overlooking a spring fed pond near a river." Indeed, the home does feature a rather horn-like prow, reflective of its name. Joseph and his wife Lois wanted a home "where we could watch the wildlife come to the water."

Wythe's studio, *Alternative Architecture*, stresses earth-sheltered design, energy-effecient organic architecture, selecting non-toxic renewable materials and systems, while developing projects to take advantage of the building site's various natural conditions.

"The home is an expression of my architectural philosophy," he says, "human scale, space modeling, the continuous present, a symphony of harmonious materials at one with its surroundings, the surprising discovery of new delights."

ARCHITECT & BUILDER: JOSEPH HENRY WYTHE - SANDPOINT, ID

*W*ythe's approach to architectural design includes designing systems for heating, cooling, ventilation, plumbing, and lighting to be non-polluting, efficient, effective, and easily controlled, using—as much as possible—renewable resources: Sun, wind, water, and vegetation.

The respected architect enjoys exploring the existing spaces and energy conservation possible with earth sheltered design.

The Hetland House

Photography by Phil McClain

The Hetland home perches in the Boise foothills overlooking Hulls Gulch offering a panoramic view of the Treasure Valley. This southwestern-styled gem is a three-story structure built by J Bar K and Associates that combines the elements of shape, color and texture to achieve its overall effect. The grand entrance hall features a mosaic tile "rug" accented by rich, warm walls. Recessed shelving built in with curves and flowing lines provides natural frameworks for books and the artwork that adorns the home. The colors of local artist Tony Ball feature sunrises and sunsets that enhance the southwest décor.

ARCHITECT: SCOTT KAMM - BOISE, ID
BUILDER: J BAR K - EAGLE, ID

Bottom: The backyard landscape capitalizes on the southwestern theme with its curving swimming pool accentuated by low-growing shrubbery, a slate walk and stonework.

The exterior of the home is a study in the clean lines of southwestern architecture accentuated by the graceful curve of the turret and the subtle rise of the three stories.

The House at
Eagle's Perch

*E*agle's Perch, constructed of quarried sandstone from the Idaho foothills, is nestled on five acres of the banks of the Boise River. The fifty-foot roof of thatched cedar shake rises above the landscaped estate with raised rock gardens, quarried sandstone rose gardens and fifty-foot cottonwood, Russian olive and copper rose trees.

The home features nine-foot pewter doors, limestone flooring, eighteen-foot arched windows and a magnificent free-hanging spiral staircase. With 13,000 square feet of living space, this elegant home offers a Great Room featuring the *Eagle's Perch on the River* sculpture, an oak-paneled library, a formal dining room with silk wall coverings, a 500-bottle-storage wine cellar, a master bedroom with a Brazilian black granite fireplace and a 30 x 50 foot recreation room overlooking the stream and river below. The grounds boast a vine-covered arbor, high-tech greenhouse and custom-engineered streams and ponds that attract nesting bald eagles.

The kitchen is a gourmet's dream with a six-by-ten foot granite island and a custom oak china hutch with beveled glass doors accented by the polished slat oak flooring. A charming view of the stone and herringbone tile bi-level patio is offered through the nine-foot bay window in the breakfast nook.

A magnificent fourteen-foot stone and granite fireplace with a custom oak mantel warms the family room with its coffered oak ceilings and fabric and oak wall coverings.

Photography by Phil McClain

ARCHITECT: BRS ARCHITECTS - BOISE, ID
BUILDER: RANDY HEMMER - BOISE, ID

Like the eagles that perch nearby, the English Tudor house sits grandly on the Boise River. Architect Tim Terry's design concept captured the site's main feature "the Boise River" by incorporating a lineal designed floor plan. By reflecting the lineal nature of the river, the house invites views to the river from every room.

"It took a team effort with the architect, owners, interior designer and my crews to create this one of a kind, timeless estate. It was a wonderful experience," says builder Randy Hemmer of Randy Hemmer Construction L.L.C.

Inside the solid pewter doors of Eagle's Perch are the traditional trappings of elegance—towering ceilings, a spiral staircase, (opposite far left) and brilliant oriental rugs. With the desire to entertain large groups of people, the design utilizes wide corridors linking all the main living areas. The main living room displays enormous glass and concrete artwork by Laddie John Dill.

There is unique intergrated roof venting within the random shake-styled roof and separate, complete groundskeepers quarters over the garage. Locally quarried sandstone is used internally and externally.

The Villelli House

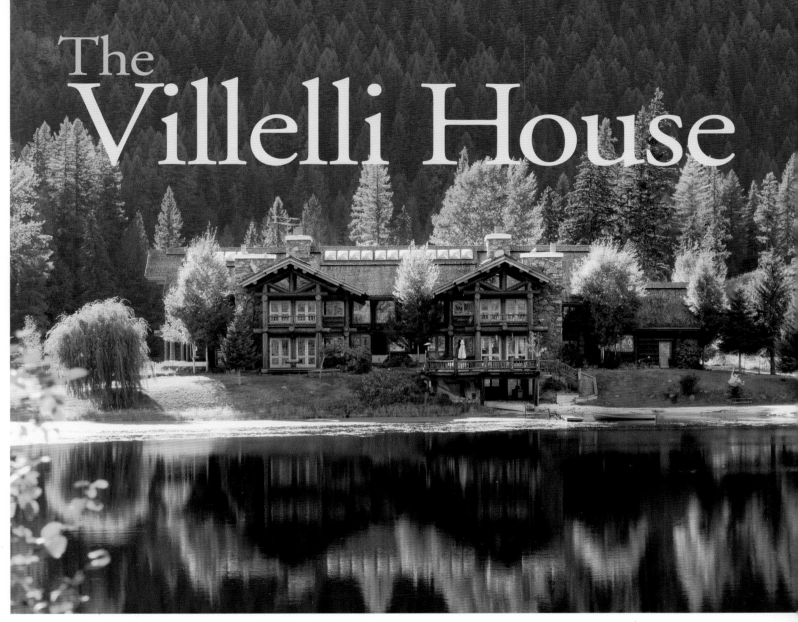

B O N N E R ' S   F E R R Y , I D A H O

Photography by Quicksilver Studios

The Villelli House, located at the tip of the Idaho panhandle, was once considered to be the largest log home in North America at 21,000 square feet. The location gives quick access to world-class skiing, water sports, golf and other outdoor activities. Constructed wholly of native western larch logs and local stone, it sits gracefully amidst 135 acres of pasture and timberland. The property features a private lake, two streams, and a plethora of wildlife, including elk, deer, bear, eagles and osprey. The main floor features a Great Room with a stone-lined grand entranceway and stone fireplaces at either end that rise thirty feet. On one end of the great room is an office, a full greenhouse, a main guest room, and on the other is the kitchen, breakfast nook, pantry, and utility room.

ARCHITECTS: MCLAUGHLIN & ASSOCIATES-
SUN VALLEY, ID
BUILDER: CLARENCE STILWILL-
SUN VALLEY, ID

The kitchen, with Spanish-tiled flooring, offers the gourmand an octagonal cooking island and restaurant-grade appliances, a brick pizza oven, a wood range and many other features.

The second floor has six bedroom suites with private baths, fireplaces, and outside decks.

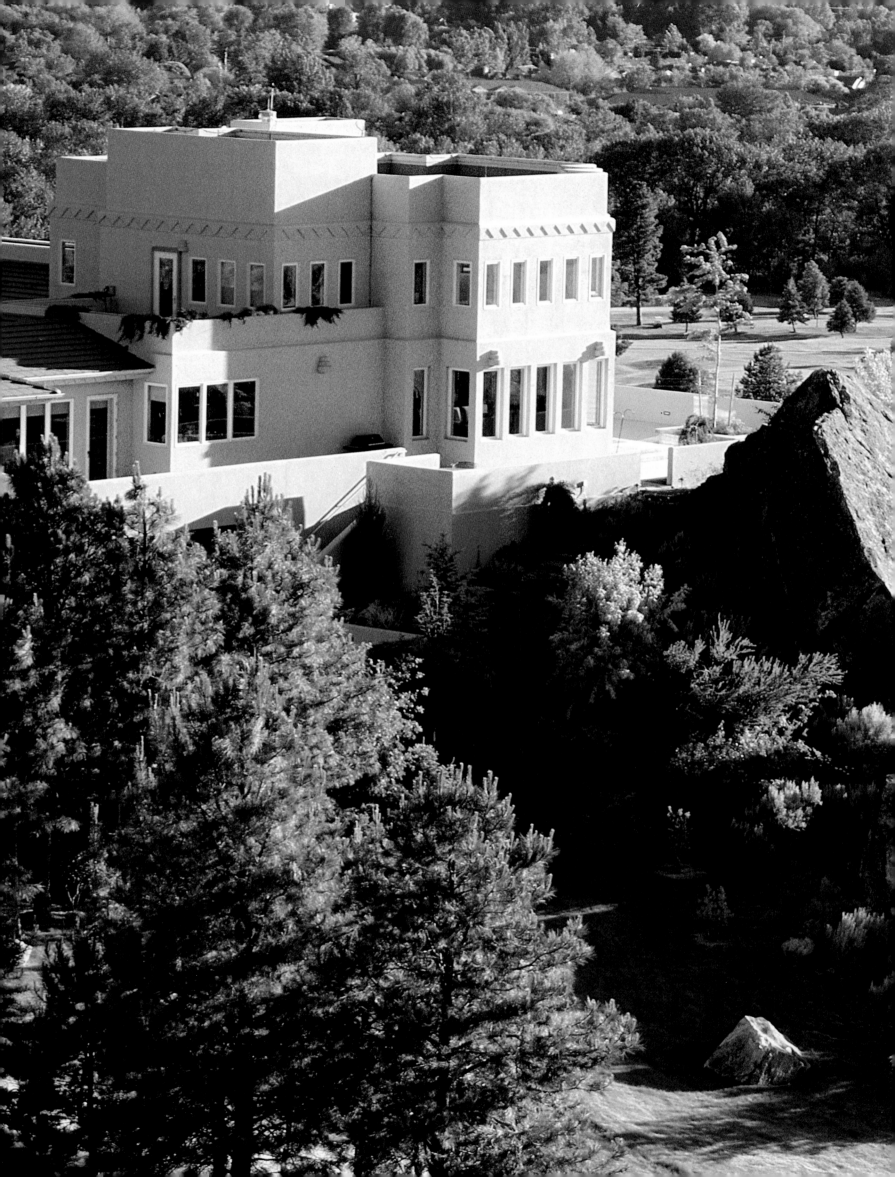

The House above Warm Springs

BOISE, IDAHO
Photography by Phil McClain

The Satz House sits on a small plateau overlooking Warm Springs Golf Course in Boise. The river winds below while the southwest plains and distant mountains complete the view. A paved drive welcomes guests to their first view of the house with built-in planters splashing color against the off-white exterior. From the entryway its possible to step down into an intimate theater and billiard room or ascend a magnificent stair tower. The floating stairway is sculpted of winding maple treads with landings at each corner, that leads to the main living area above, and a private office on the third floor. The main level is stunning with its twenty-foot ceilings, Mayan design motifs, individual windows and flat roof. The grand room is set between two enormous basalt rocks that anchor the central living area to the hillside. On the north side of the grand room is a gourmet kitchen with north- and east-facing windows and a breakfast nook.

ARCHITECT:
TREY HOFF
BOISE, ID
BUILDER:
VISSER BUILDING
CO. - BOISE, ID

The entire house is finished in stucco plaster, blending the natural colors of the soil and rocks.

One of the most delightful features in the kitchen is a dumbwaiter that transports groceries from the lower level or delivers snacks to the private office.

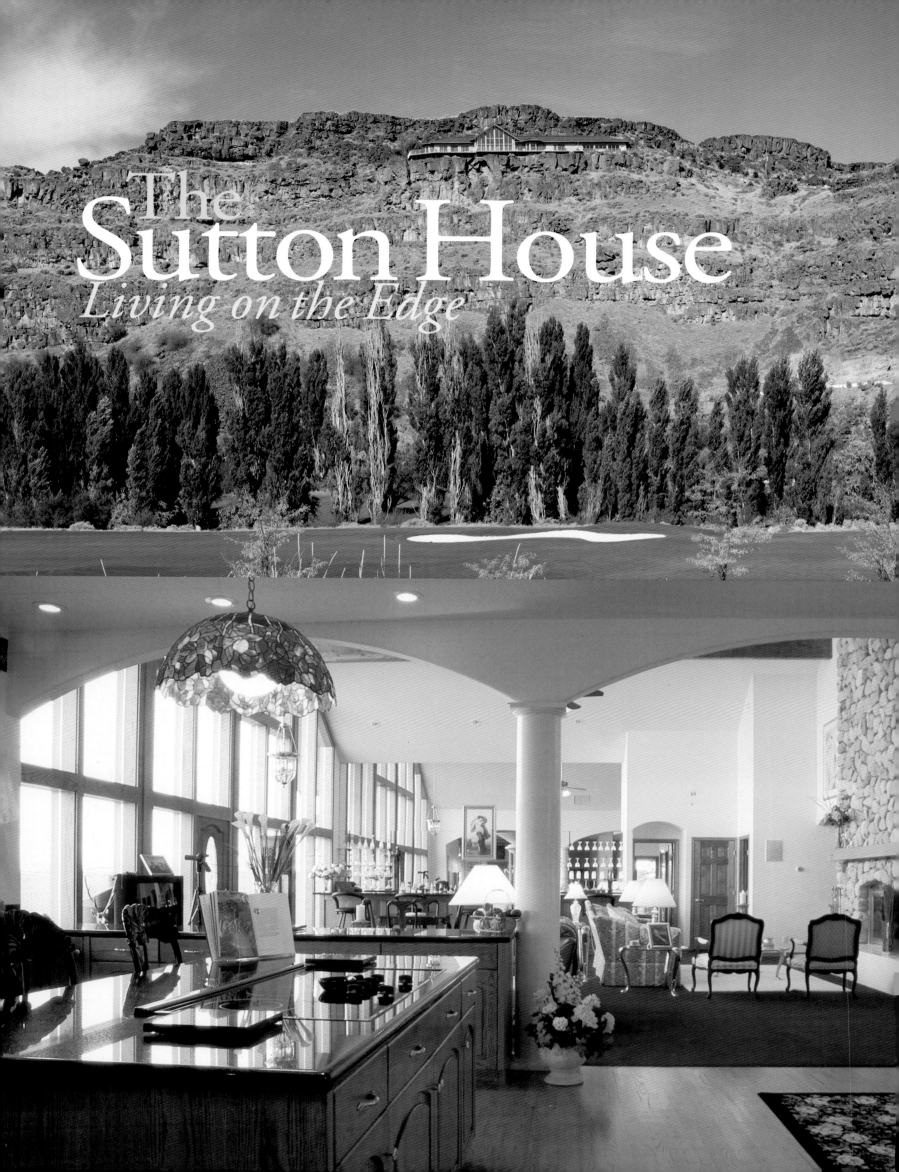

The Sutton House
Living on the Edge

TWIN FALLS, IDAHO

Photography by Tim Brown & Lisa Brown

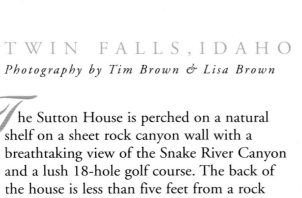

The Sutton House is perched on a natural shelf on a sheet rock canyon wall with a breathtaking view of the Snake River Canyon and a lush 18-hole golf course. The back of the house is less than five feet from a rock wall that adds drama to the decking that surrounds the front and south sides of the home. This house truly epitomizes the phrase, "Location, location, location," with its spectacular views of the Twin Falls area.

Close by is Shoshone Falls, which stretches 1,000 feet across the Snake River and is known as the Niagara of the West because its 212-foot height is 40 feet higher than Niagara Falls.

Created 15,000 years ago by the great Bonneville Flood, Shoshone Falls thunders in the springtime with the roar of its white cascade of water heard three miles away.

The Snake River canyon was made famous in 1974, when daredevil Evil Knievel mesmerized the world with his attempted rocket-powered motorcycle leap across the canyon, near the town of Twin Falls. Knievel's launching ramp still stands to the east of Perrine Bridge, as does the spot where he parachuted to the edge of the river on the canyon floor.

Not far away are the 1500-foot-long Perrine Bridge and the new and beautiful Centennial Waterfront Park some 500 feet below. Other highlights of the view include two of Idaho's most beautiful golf courses.

Views are spectacular from the south and east sides with over 400 square feet of glass in the great room alone. The house is situated approximately 50 feet down from the top of the rock wall and 400 feet above the canyon floor.

DESIGNER: EVE SIMON - TWIN FALLS, ID
BUILDER: GARY BOND - TWIN FALLS, ID

Construction of this home was a unique challenge involving blasting uphill from the shelf to allow room for the house and using heavy equipment to remove the loose boulders. Since the site could only be accessed from one side, construction was

done in four stages: The master suite completed floor to roof, then the great room, followed by the kitchen and dining area and the three bedrooms, and concluding with the garage at the widest part of the shelf at 40 feet.

This unique home becomes one with the landscape as it takes advantage of the natural beauty of the desert, river and canyon, complemented by the artful design of the golf course below.

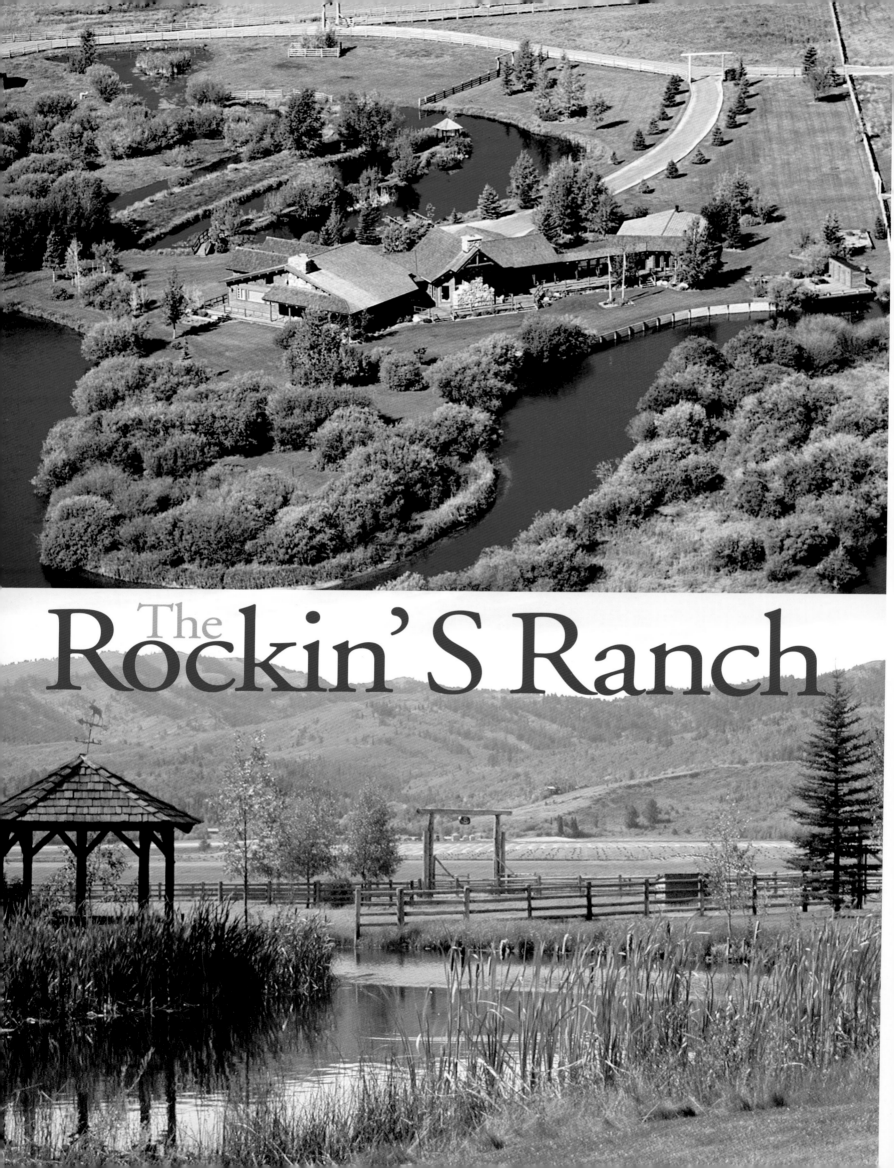

The Rockin'S Ranch

The Rockin' S Ranch blends into the banks of the Teton River known for its remarkable fly-fishing and features a wide deck around the entire house that offers views of the soaring Teton Mountain Range. With nearly a half mile of river frontage and a boathouse and dock just 30 yards from the main house, the home offers easy access to water sports. Situated on 5 secluded acres, the property also offers lush landscape and several stocked ponds. The 6,400-square-foot home is constructed of hand-peeled logs, which have been tempered for over a century. The beams add historical beauty to the windows, doorways, and mantels throughout the home. The main house features a dramatic great room with two river rock fireplaces that vault to the ceilings. The spacious kitchen and dining area offer casual and comfortable amenities. The house also has four guest rooms with private baths, a loft area, and a unique, handcrafted log billiards table.

ARCHITECT: FRED BABCOCK - SALT LAKE CITY, UT
BUILDER: DONN SAINDON & BEARD CONSTRUCTION - DRIGGS, ID

Above: The ranch features a 5,000-square-foot barn and riding arena. The upper level serves as an additional guest house.

173

The Drackett House

The high ceilings and the warm tones of the decor create an inviting atmosphere at the Drackett House.

Barns supplied by The Barn People - Woodstock, Vermont.

Photography by Kevin Syms

This unique home in the Wood River Valley is constructed of five, 200-year-old Vermont barns, which were dismantled and relocated to the Sun Valley area, making it the oldest building in Idaho. The entrance of the Drackett Barns features a heavy alder door that passes into a sunny gallery hallway. To the right is the living room complete with a European fireplace, flanked by floor-to-ceiling bookshelves. The room's warm feel is created with the cinnamon-colored barn-board ceiling that is supported by hand-hewn white oak beams. Beyond the living room is the master suite accented with oversized furniture and wonderful views through the well-placed windows. A children's hall, formerly a dairy barn, includes four rooms that surround a dramatic common room. The kitchen and dining room feature trusses salvaged from an antique barn in Canada. The countertops are Baltic brown granite and the round dining table easily seats ten. The garage, which has an upstairs office and also serves as a covered walkway to the Orwell Barn with separate living quarters, was a four-bay livery stable.

ARCHITECT: DAMIAN FERRELL GROUP - ANN ARBOR, MI
BUILDER: JACK MCNAMARA - KETCHUM, ID

BOISE, IDAHO

The Comstock Townhouse overlooks the city of Boise from the top floor of the Washington Mutual building. The condominium, at just over 2,300 square feet, is a unique accomplishment in melding the look and feel of old and new world styles to provide a true metropolitan experience. It is finished with a natural palette of materials, and the designer's eye for detail was critical to finessing everything from craftsmanship to colors in this relatively small space with an expansive feel.

The entryway to the two-story loft home gives way to the kitchen, which is styled after a restaurant on a quaint Italian street. This ambience is accented by a charming table for two and marble countertops (crafted from the same marble used in the Washington Monument) and limestone treatments. From the kitchen, the hallway

Photography by Phil McClain

DESIGNER: ROBERT COMSTOCK - BOISE, ID
BUILDER: W.R. GANN - BOISE, ID

creates a passage from the Mediterranean theme to that of a New York loft. This was accomplished with the use of a railing that gives way

to mottled lath and plaster wall as one climbs the stairs to a surprising indoor garden area. The garden was specially created by the designer (who planned the house as a residence for his mother) to bring his mother's fondness for gardening indoors. The matching brick flooring carries out the outdoor patio garden theme.

The details in the house are all natural in feel from the old-style lath and plaster walls to the three types of maple—including a winter-cut maple used for its different hue—to the walls finished with a buttery-velvet texture.

UPTOWN LIVING
The Leasure Residence at
The Grove Hotel

Photography by Tom Stewart

BOISE, IDAHO

The Grove Hotel complex includes a hockey rink and concert venue, and provides easy access to downtown events and attractions. Sitting atop the Grove Hotel are four floors of luxury condominiums reminiscent of the grand hotels on the east coast. Wrapped around the south end of the hotel, overlooking downtown Boise is the Leasure home. The home features six rooms including a library and media room. The entry boasts two antique pillars from Thailand and the ceiling soffet contains four double-fortune Chinese symbols. The living room is open and expansive with maple flooring and a custom cherry wood fireplace. An eclectic mix of antique furnishings and modern artwork add warmth to the formal room. The dining room features a mural flanked by two victory Angels and the handpainted silk chandelier is from Fortuny, Italy. The warm and inviting library adjoining the living room is the perfect place to snuggle up with a good book in the suede leather chair.

ARCHITECT: HNTB - BELLEVUE, WA
BUILDER: PCL CONSTRUCTION - BELLEVUE, WA

At right: The focal point of the master bedroom is a large four-poster bed and abstract oil by a local artist. Top: A cozy fireside chaise and silk and satin draperies finish the room.

The kitchen, with etched concrete floors, granite counters and a custom leather banquet and table, connects the formal and informal wings of the home.

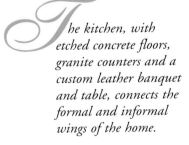

Idaho

Published by RHINO BOOKS

P.O. Box 16348 Boise, ID 83715 *www.RhinoBooks.net*

• *To obtain limited edition fine art prints or use of many of the images in this book go to www.bigtreeseditions.com*
Photos in this book are protected by copyright.
• *For additional copies contact RHINO BOOKS*
www.RhinoBooks.Net